AMAZING ADVENTURES

TO SPACE

WRITTEN BY
ALEX HALL

All rights reserved.
Printed in India.

A catalogue record for this book is available from the British Library.

ISBN: 978-1-80505-602-7

Written by:
Alex Hall

Edited by:
Rebecca Phillips-Bartlett

Designed by:
Ker Ker Lee

©2024
BookLife Publishing Ltd.
King's Lynn, Norfolk
PE30 4LS, UK

MIX
Paper | Supporting responsible forestry
FSC® C195953

All facts, statistics, web addresses and URLs in this book were verified as valid and accurate at time of writing. No responsibility for any changes to external websites or references can be accepted by either the author or publisher.

AN INTRODUCTION TO BOOKLIFE RAPID READERS...

Packed full of gripping topics and twisted tales, BookLife Rapid Readers are perfect for older children looking to propel their reading up to top speed. With three levels based on our planet's fastest animals, children will be able to find the perfect point from which to accelerate their reading journey. From the spooky to the silly, these roaring reads will turn every child at every reading level into a prolific page-turner!

CHEETAH
The fastest animals on land, cheetahs will be taking their first strides as they race to top speed.

MARLIN
The fastest animals under water, marlins will be blasting through their journey.

FALCON
The fastest animals in the air, falcons will be flying at top speed as they tear through the skies.

Contents

PAGE 4	Your Journey to Space
PAGE 6	Yuri Gagarin
PAGE 8	Valentina Tereshkova
PAGE 12	Alexei Leonov
PAGE 14	Neil Armstrong and Buzz Aldrin
PAGE 18	Guion Bluford
PAGE 22	Kathryn Sullivan
PAGE 24	Susan Helms
PAGE 26	Valeri Vladimirovich Polyakov
PAGE 30	Where Will Your Journey in Space Take You?
PAGE 31	Glossary
PAGE 32	Index

Words that look like <u>this</u> are explained in the glossary on page 31.

YOUR JOURNEY TO SPACE

This is ground control speaking. This mission will be heading out of this world to follow some of space's most amazing explorers.

Space can be dangerous if you are not prepared. So, make sure to wear a spacesuit.

We will be flying rocket ships, floating in space and walking on the Moon. Prepare for blast off.

Are you ready to begin your journey into space? It will take your breath away!

Yuri Gagarin

1934–1968

Our space journey begins with a cosmonaut called Yuri Gagarin. A cosmonaut is a Russian space explorer.

In 1961, Gagarin became the first person to go into space. Gagarin went around Earth in less than two hours.

Gagarin's spacecraft was designed to break apart in space on the way back to Earth. He had to parachute to the ground to land safely.

Gagarin's journey to space was important for helping humans understand space.

GAGARIN'S CAPSULE AND SPACESUIT

Valentina Tereshkova

As a young woman, Valentina Tereshkova spent many hours parachuting on Earth. Her parachuting experience got her chosen for cosmonaut training.

She trained for a year and a half before she could go into space.

1937

In 1963, Tereshkova became the first woman to ever go into space. She travelled in a spacecraft called Vostok 6.

TERESHKOVA'S SPACECRAFT

She spent nearly three days orbiting Earth. She went around the planet a total of 48 times.

Tereshkova did have some problems on her journey. Tereshkova had plenty of food, drinks and toothpaste... but no toothbrush! She had to brush her teeth with her finger.

Her second problem was more serious.

Tereshkova's spacecraft was not <u>programmed</u> to go back down to Earth. Luckily, Tereshkova noticed the issue and asked ground control to fix it.

Tereshkova returned safely to Earth and became the first woman to complete a solo mission to space.

Alexei Leonov
1934-2019

Are you ready to step out of the spacecraft? Alexei Leonov was a cosmonaut and the first person to go on a spacewalk.

He needed a special suit to breathe because there is no air in space.

After 12 minutes of walking in space, Leonov noticed a problem with his spacesuit.

His spacesuit had swollen up with too much air to fit back into the spacecraft. He had to let out air to get back inside.

Neil Armstrong and Buzz Aldrin

1930–2012

Neil Armstrong and Buzz Aldrin were American astronauts. These two walked where no one had walked before.

NEIL ARMSTRONG

BUZZ ALDRIN

1930

In 1969, Armstrong and Aldrin were part of the American mission to be the first country to land on the Moon.

Michael Collins was the third astronaut on the mission.

MICHAEL COLLINS

Armstrong became the first man to walk on the Moon, and Aldrin was the second. Collins stayed in the spacecraft to make sure they could get back safely.

Around 650 million people watched Armstrong take his first steps on the Moon's surface.

Armstrong and Aldrin collected some information about the Moon. Scientists used this information to learn more about the Moon when they returned to Earth.

Armstrong and Aldrin travelled a total of 250 metres on the Moon's surface and spent over 21 hours there.

Armstrong and Aldrin will forever be remembered in history for doing something that no other humans had ever done.

Guion Bluford

1942

Our next space explorer is an American astronaut called Guion Bluford. Before he became an astronaut, Bluford trained as a fighter pilot in the United States Air Force.

Bluford was chosen out of 10,000 people to become an astronaut.

In 1983, Bluford made history by becoming the first African American astronaut in space. He flew above Earth aboard a spacecraft called the Challenger.

Bluford helped with multiple experiments by collecting information about space.

Bluford was also the first African American astronaut to return to space for a second, third and fourth time when he flew to space in 1985, 1991 and 1992.

Bluford spent a total of 688 hours in space.

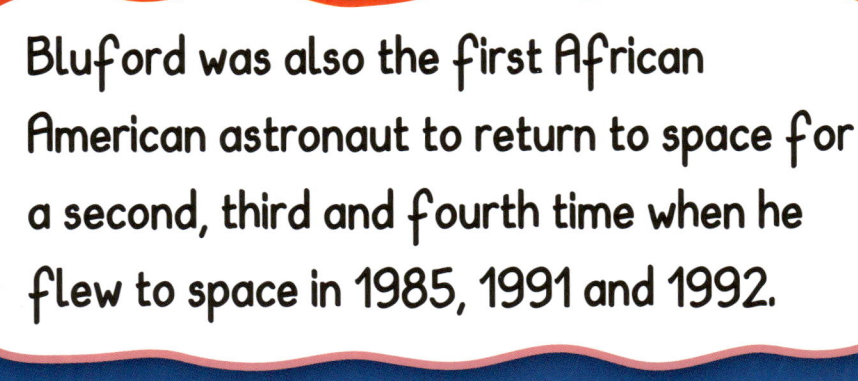

Bluford led the research into many important space inventions.

Bluford wanted his adventures in space to be an inspiration for other people. He tried to encourage other African American people to go to space too.

Kathryn Sullivan

1951

Kathryn Sullivan explored the extremes of low and high. As an <u>oceanographer</u>, Sullivan explored the Mariana Trench. The Mariana Trench is the deepest part of the ocean.

As an astronaut, Sullivan flew on three journeys to space.

Sullivan became the first woman to go on a spacewalk.

She also helped to launch the Hubble Space Telescope. The telescope is used to photograph parts of space that are too far away to see from Earth.

HUBBLE SPACE TELESCOPE

Susan Helms

1958

Our next spaceflight journey is with Susan Helms. Helms worked as an American astronaut and Air Force officer.

Helms helped make repairs to the International Space Station. She later went back to live there as part of its second crew.

In 2001, Helms performed a spacewalk for nearly nine hours with another astronaut called James Voss. They broke the record for the longest spacewalk.

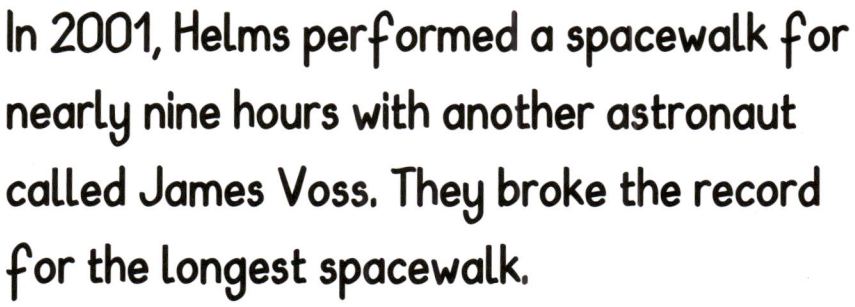

Helms spent 163 days aboard the International Space Station and 211 days in space.

Valeri Vladimirovich Polyakov

1942–2022

Valeri Vladimirovich Polyakov was a cosmonaut. In 1994, Polyakov was launched into space. He lived on a space station by himself.

On the space station, he studied how space affects the human body.

Polyakov spent almost 438 days in space in one journey. During that time, he went around Earth over 7,000 times. Polyakov broke the record for the longest time spent in space at one time.

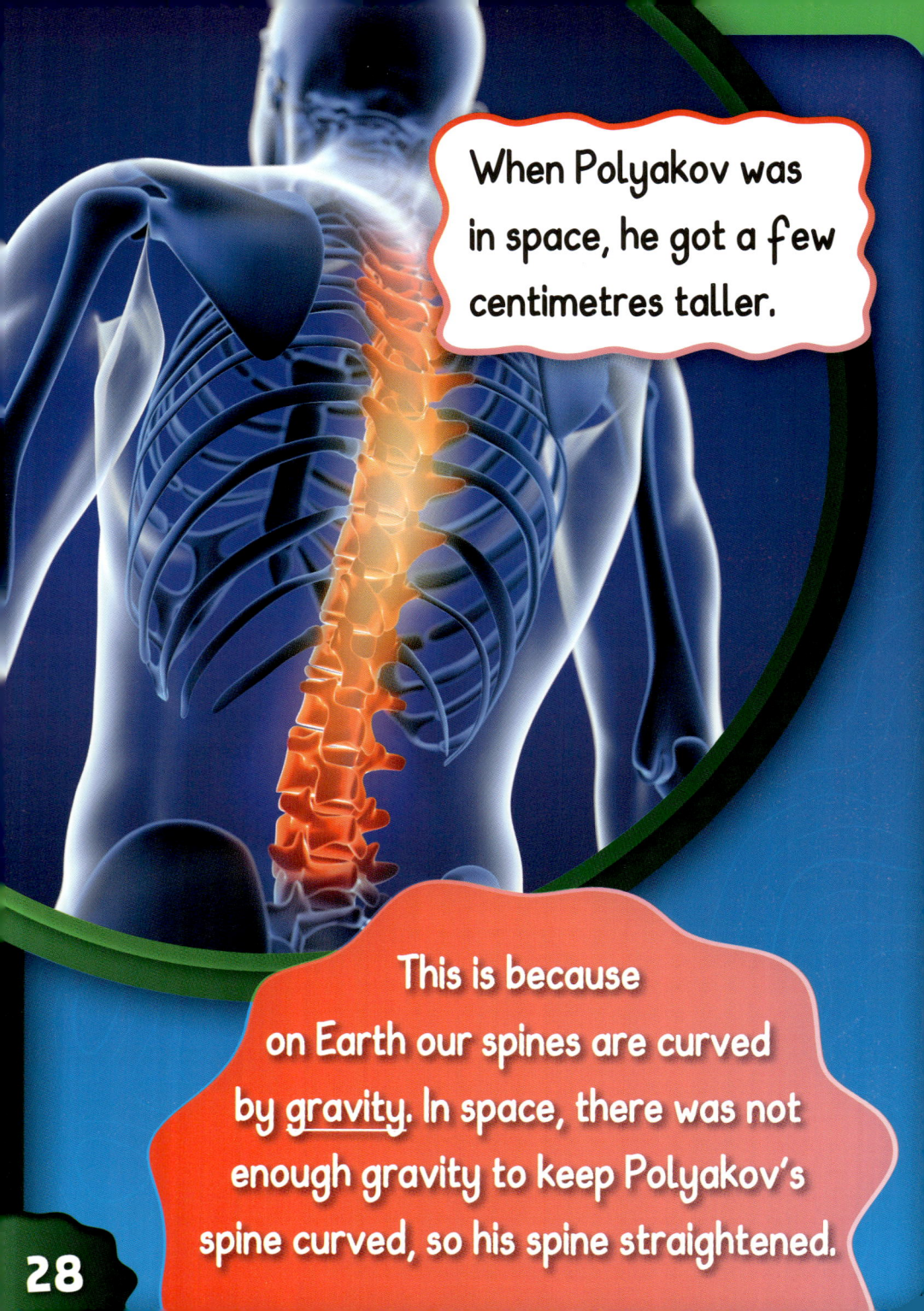

When Polyakov returned to Earth, he was still able to walk after a long time in low gravity.

This proved that humans could stay mostly healthy in space for a long time and could survive a long journey to Mars.

Where will your journey in Space take you?

What an exciting journey in space! You have done an amazing job.

There is so much more to discover in space. People are still trying to explore it today. Will you be blasting off with them too?

INDEX

air 12–13, 18, 24

Earth 6–9, 11, 16, 19, 23, 27–29

fingers 10

humans 7, 17, 26, 29

Moon, the 5, 14–17

scientists 16

spacesuits 4, 7, 13

spines 28

teeth 10

telescopes 23

Photo Credits – Images are courtesy of Shutterstock.com. With thanks to Getty Images, Thinkstock Photo and iStockphoto.
Recurring images – Elena Pimukova, Svetolk, Dancake. Cover – Dima Zel, Castleski. 4–5 – Artsiom P, Vadim Sadovski. 6–7 – greenacre8, CC BY 2.0 <https://creativecommons.org/licenses/by/2.0>, via Wikimedia Commons. 8–9 – Scifier, RIA Novosti archive, image #612748 / Alexander Mokletsov / CC-BY-SA 3.0, CC BY-SA 3.0 <https://creativecommons.org/licenses/by-sa/3.0>, via Wikimedia Commons. 10–11 – A.Savin, CC BY-SA 3.0 <https://creativecommons.org/licenses/by-sa/3.0/>, via Wikimedia Commons. 12–13 – Memorial Museum of Astronautics, CC BY-SA 3.0 <https://creativecommons.org/licenses/by-sa/3.0>, via Wikimedia Common. 16–17 – Beth Morley. 26–27 – Mil.ru, CC BY 4.0 <https://creativecommons.org/licenses/by/4.0>, via Wikimedia Commons. 28–29 – cla78, Vadim Sadovski. 30 – IM_photo.

GLOSSARY

astronauts	people who have learnt how to travel in space
gravity	the force that pulls everything downwards towards the centre of large objects in space, such as Earth
ground control	the people and things that help with planning the flight and landing of aircraft or spacecraft
International Space Station	a large spacecraft where some astronauts live to study space
oceanographer	a scientist who explores and studies the ocean
orbiting	travelling around something in space
parachute	to jump or drop from an aircraft wearing a sheet of cloth, called a parachute, to slow the fall
programmed	the instructions that have told a computer what to do
spacecraft	a vehicle used to transport people or things in space
spacewalk	when an astronaut does things in space outside a spacecraft